Forever Grateful To You:

Made in the USA
Las Vegas, NV
13 December 2022

62358150R00061